CountryMusic ★ Stars

SUGARLAND

By Bret Jemaine

Gareth Stevens
Publishing

Please visit our Web site, www.garethstevens.com. For a free color catalog of all our high-quality books, call toll free 1-800-542-2595 or fax 1-877-542-2596.

Library of Congress Cataloging-in-Publication Data

Jemaine, Bret.
  Sugarland / Bret Jemaine.
      p. cm. —(Country music stars)
  Includes index.
  ISBN 978-1-4339-3939-6 (pbk.)
  ISBN 978-1-4339-3940-2 (6-pack)
  ISBN 978-1-4339-3938-9 (library binding)
  1. Sugarland (Musical group)—Juvenile literature. 2. Country musicians—United States—Biography—Juvenile literature. I. Title.
  ML3930.S93J45 2010
  782.421642092'2-—dc22

  [B]
                                        2010007165

First Edition

Published in 2011 by
Gareth Stevens Publishing
111 East 14th Street, Suite 349
New York, NY 10003

Designer: Haley W. Harasymiw
Editor: Therese Shea

Photo credits: Cover background Shutterstock.com; cover, p. 1 Frazer Harrison/Getty Images; pp. 5, 9, 23 Rick Diamond/Getty Images; pp. 7, 15, 21 Scott Gries/Getty Images; p. 11 Kevin Winter/Getty Images; pp. 13, 19 Evan Agostini/Getty Images; p. 17 Frederick M. Brown/Getty Images; pp. 25, 27 Ethan Miller/Getty Images; p. 29 Jason Merritt/Getty Images.

Printed in the United States of America

CPSIA compliance information: Batch #CS10GS: For further information contact Gareth Stevens, New York, New York at 1-800-542-2595.

CONTENTS

CHANGING BAND

Sugarland is a country music band with two members. However, the band began with three members.

HOW IT BEGAN

Kristen Hall was a musician living in Atlanta, Georgia. In 2003, she wanted to try something new.

Kristen asked Kristian Bush to form a band with her. They called the band Sugarland.

Jennifer Nettles was a singer in Atlanta. Kristen and Kristian asked her to be Sugarland's lead singer.

The three members of Sugarland

knew they had a special sound.

One of their first songs was called

"Baby Girl."

SWEET SUCCESS

Four months after the band formed,
Sugarland performed their first
concert. The crowd loved them!

A record company asked Sugarland to make an album. They called it *Twice the Speed of Life*. Sugarland won an award for best new artist.

THE SONGS GO ON

In 2006, Kristen Hall decided to leave Sugarland. The band was now just Jennifer and Kristian.

Kristian and Jennifer's second album was called *Enjoy the Ride*. Jennifer also had a hit song with Bon Jovi. It was called "Who Says You Can't Go Home."

Jon Bon Jovi

21

Sugarland won awards for their song "Stay." It was the first Sugarland song that Jennifer wrote alone.

23

MORE SWEET SONGS

Many music stars have performed with Sugarland. Here is the band with Beyoncé.

Beyoncé

Sugarland performed with the band Brooks & Dunn. They played with Taylor Swift, too!

Kix Brooks

Ronnie Dunn

Taylor Swift

Sugarland's third album was called *Love on the Inside.* It had three number-one songs!

TIMELINE

2003   Kristen Hall, Kristian Bush, and Jennifer Nettles form Sugarland.

2004   Sugarland makes their first album.

2005   Sugarland wins an award for best new artist.

2006   Kristen Hall leaves Sugarland.

2006   Sugarland puts out their second album.

2008   Sugarland puts out their third album.

2009   Sugarland's song "Stay" wins an award for best country song.

FOR MORE INFORMATION

Books:

Bertholf, Bret. *The Long Gone Lonesome History of Country Music.* New York, NY: Little, Brown and Company, 2007.

Riggs, Kate. *Country Music.* Mankato, MN: Creative Education, 2008.

Web Sites:

CMT.com: Sugarland

www.cmt.com/artists/az/sugarland/bio.jhtml

Sugarland: Meet the Band

www.sugarlandmusic.com/band.aspx

GLOSSARY

award: a prize given to someone for doing something well

concert: a public music event

musician: someone who plays, sings, or writes music

perform: to play or sing a piece of music

record company: a business that produces and sells music

INDEX